HOORAY FOR DENTISTS!

by Tessa Kenan

BUMBA BOOKS™

LERNER PUBLICATIONS ◆ MINNEAPOLIS

Note to Educators:

Throughout this book, you'll find critical thinking questions. These can be used to engage young readers in thinking critically about the topic and in using the text and photos to do so.

Lerner Publications Company
A division of Lerner Publishing Group, Inc.
241 First Avenue North
Minneapolis, MN 55401 USA

For reading levels and more information, look up this title at www.lernerbooks.com.

Library of Congress Cataloging-in-Publication Data

Names: Kenan, Tessa, author.
Title: Hooray for dentists! / by Tessa Kenan.
Description: Minneapolis : Lerner Publications, [2018] | Series: Bumba books. Hooray for community helpers! | Audience: Age 4–7. | Audience: K to Grade 3. | Includes bibliographical references and index.
Identifiers: LCCN 2016044350 (print) | LCCN 2016044526 (ebook) | ISBN 9781512433517 (lb : alk. paper) | ISBN 9781512455496 (pb : alk. paper) | ISBN 9781512450316 (eb pdf)
Subjects: LCSH: Dentists—Juvenile literature. | Teeth—Care and hygiene—Juvenile literature. | Dentistry—Vocational guidance—Juvenile literature.
Classification: LCC RK63 .K47 2018 (print) | LCC RK63 (ebook) | DDC 617.6/0232—dc23

LC record available at https://lccn.loc.gov/2016044350

Manufactured in the United States of America
1 – CG – 7/15/17

Expand learning beyond the printed book. Download free, complementary educational resources for this book from our website, www.lernerresource.com.

Table of Contents

Dentists Keep Our Teeth Healthy

Dentists care for our teeth.

They help keep our mouths healthy.

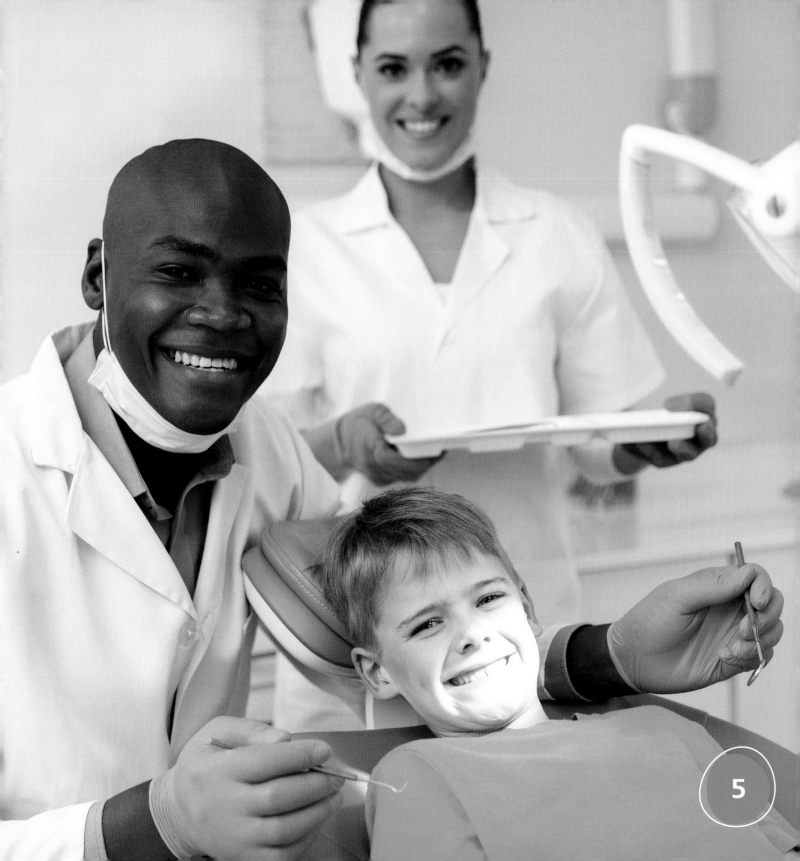

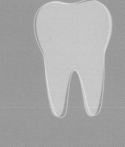

Dentists work in

special offices.

They use many tools

to check teeth.

Patients sit in a big chair.

A light helps dentists see the teeth.

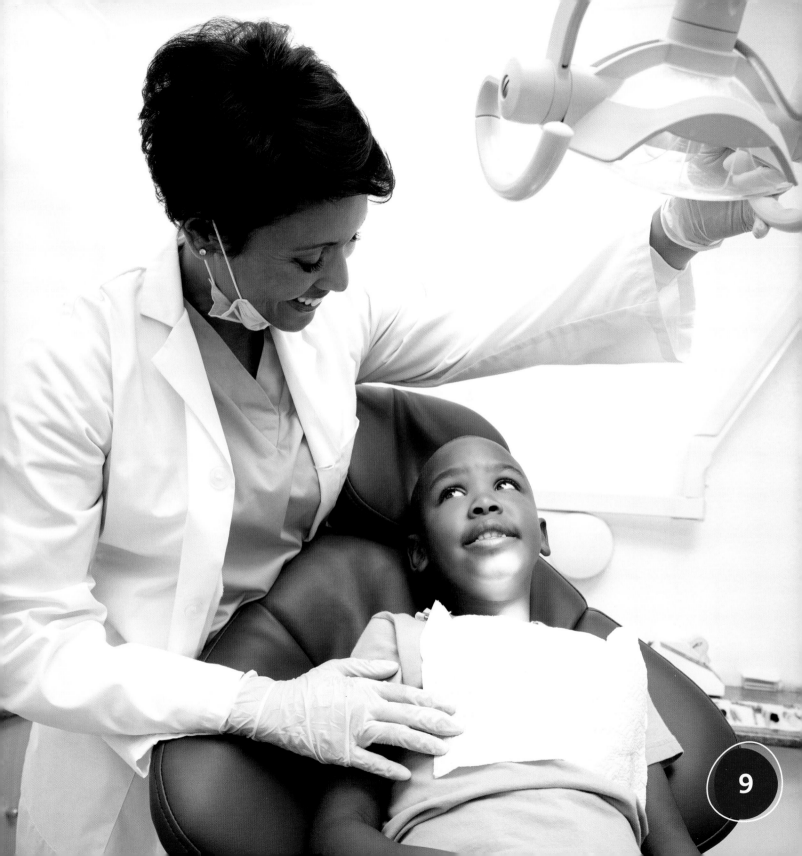

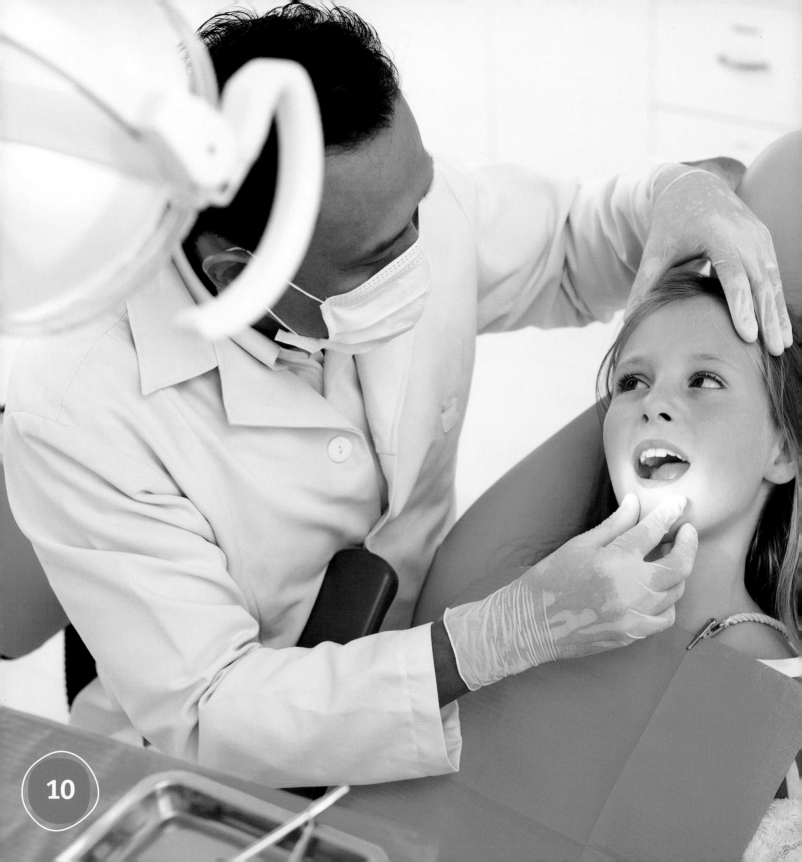

A dentist checks a

patient's mouth.

He wears gloves.

Gloves keep him and the

patient clean.

A dentist wears a mask.

Some wear scrubs.

Scrubs are a kind of uniform.

Why would dentists wear masks?

A dentist checks the patient's teeth.

She cleans them.

A dentist takes an x-ray

of teeth.

He looks for holes

in teeth.

The holes show cavities.

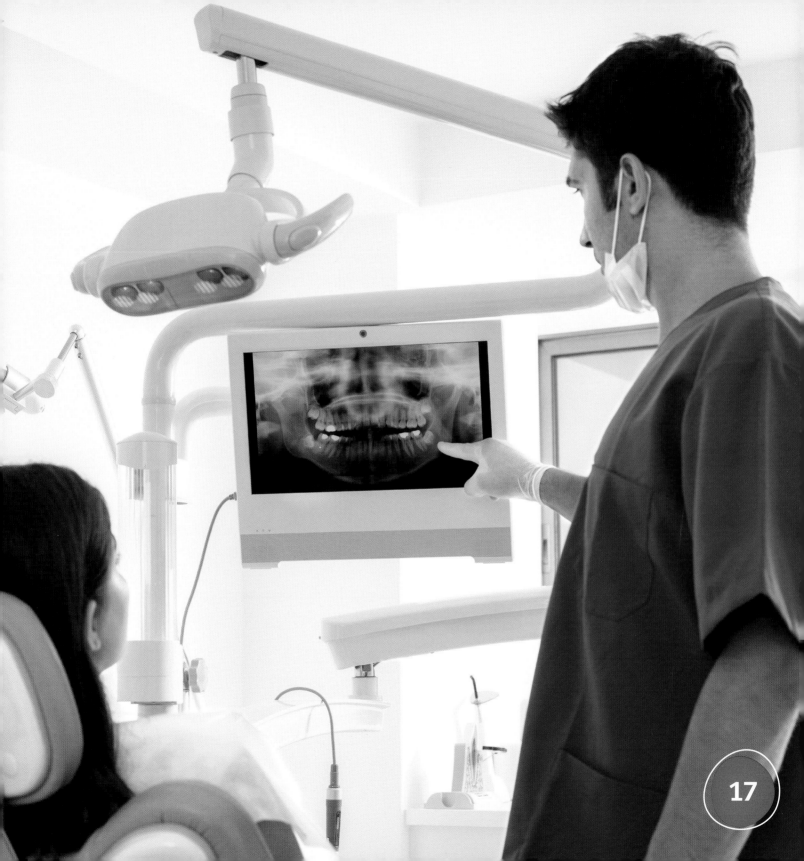

Dentists tell us about our teeth.

They show us how to keep

our teeth healthy.

How can we clean our teeth?

Dentists care about our teeth.

They give each patient a new

toothbrush.

What else might dentists give to patients?

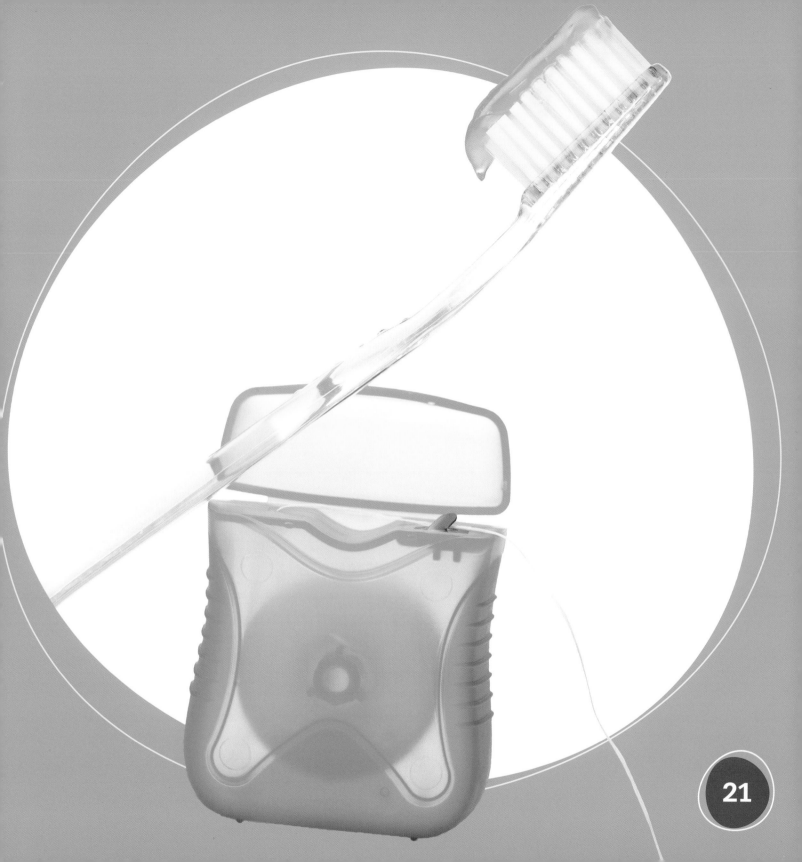

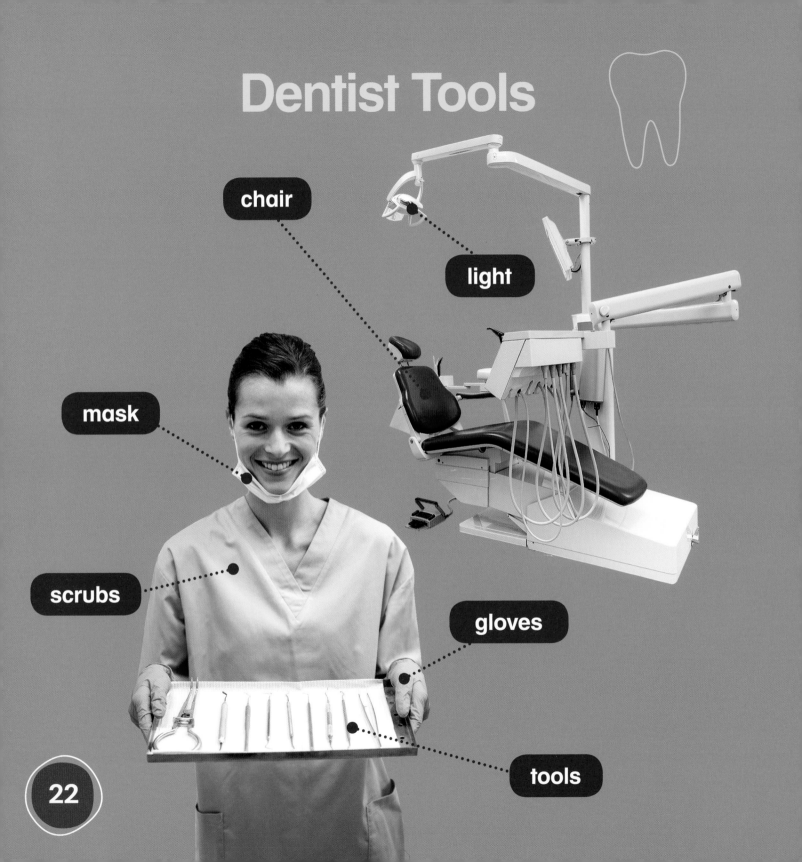

Dentist Tools

chair

light

mask

scrubs

gloves

tools

22

Picture Glossary

patients

people who receive treatment or a checkup

scrubs

uniforms dentists wear

tools

equipment dentists use to check and clean teeth

x-rays

pictures taken of teeth inside someone's mouth

Read More

Heos, Bridget. *Let's Meet a Dentist.* Minneapolis: Millbrook Press, 2013.

Hewitt, Sally. *Going to the Dentist.* Irvine, CA: QEB Publishing, 2015.

Royston, Angela. *Why Do I Brush My Teeth?* Irvine, CA: QEB Publishing, 2016.

Index

Photo Credits

The images in this book are used with the permission of: © michaeljung/iStock.com, p. 5; © Sebastian Duda/Shutterstock.com, pp. 6–7, 23 (bottom left); © Wavebreakmedia/iStock.com, pp. 9, 23 (top left); © DragonImages/iStock.com, pp. 10–11; © wavebreakmedia/Shutterstock.com, pp. 13, 22 (left), 23 (top right); © andresr/iStock.com, p. 14; © stockvisual/iStock.com, pp. 16–17, 23 (bottom right); © XiXinXing/iStock.com, p. 18; © ellobo1/iStock.com, pp. 20–21; © Photographee.eu/Shutterstock.com, p. 22 (right).

Front Cover: © Wavebreakmedia/iStock.com.